NOT *Just* A Mum

A poetic journey through motherhood and identity

Katie Gowers

For more information, email:
hello@katiegowers.co.uk.

First published in Great Britain in February 2025

ISBN 978-1-0683563-0-8 (paperback)

ISBN 978-1-0683563-1-5 (ebook)

www.katiegowers.co.uk

My Baby

I'm not sure I understood love,
so real and deep and true.
But all that changed forever,
in the moment that I met you.

Contents

Introduction

Writing, specifically writing poetry, has helped me to navigate the challenges of the last few years. In our writing group we often joke that it is the cheapest form of therapy.

This is a collection of poems about motherhood and my experience of becoming a mother for the first time. For context, I gave birth to my son a few days before the first coronavirus lockdown, hundreds of miles away from family and friends.

My journey through motherhood since then has been joyous and emotional, but also one of the most challenging things I have ever done. After eighteen months, my marriage ended suddenly, and my world changed again as I unexpectedly found myself as a single mum.

As I started to rebuild my life and find my feet, I realised I no longer knew who I was. Identity became a prominent topic in my writing and is a theme throughout this collection.

I try to be open and authentic in my writing; some poems touch on topics that could be triggers. Where possible, I have tried to include trigger warnings (TW), but because of the intensely personal nature of triggers, I know that I may have missed some, and for this, I apologise.

There have been few occasions during motherhood when I have felt truly seen. Society, in my experience, tends to sugarcoat this experience, and my intention here is to be honest and real.

There are wonderful moments as a Mum, and my son Arthur is the light of my life and the best thing that's ever happened to me.

However, there are also intense challenges, and I try to capture all aspects of parenting in my writing. I hope that someone will feel seen in the shared experiences within this collection.

Take care,

Katie x

New Mummy

I see you there, Mummy,
with your bundle small and new.
Blinking in the daylight,
the world has changed for you.

But don't forget throughout,
those hazy nights and days.
That you're surrounded by other mothers,
who can help in so many ways.

We've all been there before you.
We remember those feelings well.
So please say when you're drowning,
and we'll help you through the swell.

TW: Childbirth

Childbirth

That day, my world changed forever.
In waves of pain, blood and gore.
I had no idea until that moment,
I would lose all that I was before.

A process shrouded in mystery,
no one lets on what it's like.
No way to prepare for what's coming.
There's fear when those first contractions strike.

Months of anguish and uncertainty end,
with a plan thrown aside in a second.
I've never felt so exposed and vulnerable,
loss of control more than I'd reckoned.

Whispers of a brewing pandemic.
The risks to us all still unknown.
Isolated from loved ones by distance.
The only support from calls on my phone.

But the moment you lay on my chest,
my arms wrapped around a bundle so pure.
I knew my heart was complete in that second.
Your safety and happiness mine to secure.

I was lucky that that bond was instant,
for some, it takes a little time.
To heal from the trauma of childbirth,
and connect with the new paradigm.

The scars, both physical and mental.
No time to process them all.
A body so battered and bruised.
Thoughts spinning as if in freefall.

Childbirth is so confrontational.
It challenges everything that you have been.
And changes your life forever.
With all beliefs and values in a spin.

But it gave me the greatest of gifts,
a life with your light at the heart.
Days filled with love and laughter,
our souls spiral together from that start.

TW: Coronavirus

Born In A Pandemic

It's OK. Mum will come.
As soon as the baby is here.
Not long to wait for help,
his birth draws ever near.

I'm ten days over and desperate.
The contractions feel so strong.
My baby will finally come today.
I'm terrified it will all go wrong.

Safely home from the hospital,
but everything in the world has changed.
Rumours of a pandemic,
could ruin all plans we arranged.

Mum isn't coming anymore.
She's no longer allowed to travel.
Everyone's in lockdown suddenly.
I feel I'm starting to unravel.

I'm locked inside the house.
No one comes to meet my son.
Everyone is miles away,
I just want to see my mum.

Four and a half months later,
the restrictions are finally lifted.
I get us in a car and
some family time we all are gifted.

There's an undercurrent of anxiety,
a fear of spreading bugs.
You're still so tiny in my arms
we are unsure about giving hugs.

You were born in a global pandemic,
people dying all around.
We huddled at home together,
love and shelter sought and found.

No one knew it was coming,
how difficult it would be.
Affecting people in so many ways,
including my new baby and me.

Home From Hospital

A new bundle in my arms,
they're letting me home with you.
But I'm really not that sure,
I know what I need to do.

Walking out of the hospital,
strapping you in the car.
Reality has just caught up with me,
this is the scariest part by far.

What if you don't take my milk?
Or I can't keep you safe and warm?
How do I keep you happy, when
I feel so very far from my norm?

The pandemic is brewing around us.
We don't know what to expect.
Everyone has to stay away,
for fear they will infect.

They say it takes a village,
but we're isolated and alone.
I feel so helpless and overwhelmed,
like I'm fighting on my own.

Sometimes, you cry for hours,
and nothing that I can do
seems to make you comfortable,
I just wish I could help you.

They say I should be sleeping
when you finally do drift off.
But I sit and listen to your breath,
terrified of every cough.

TW: SIDS

Horror Story

I'm terrified of losing you,
I've heard that horror story.
A child slipping away in their sleep,
and it's there as a constant worry.

I am so completely exhausted,
but lie awake through the night.
Listening for each tiny breath,
reassuring myself that you're alright.

In My Arms

I really need a drink,
am desperate for a wee,
but you're fast asleep in my arms,
and there's nowhere I'd rather be.

Time

They grow up so fast.
That's what everybody said.
Blink and you'll miss it,
before you know it, they'll have fledged.

But nobody mentions to you,
that when they are so young.
That days last a lifetime,
and all sense of time is gone.

Sitting for hours together in a
cold and lonely room.
It feels like the world flies
rushing past in a blurry zoom.

Up half the night, and
all through the day.
It's impossible to believe,
it could be any other way.

Your entire energy focused
on keeping this tiny soul alive.
Struggling with feeding,
and hoping that they'll thrive

Now that he is older
I can barely believe,
that time has flown by suddenly
and now my little boy is three.

It's still a mystery to me,
how time works for a mum.
Years pass by so fast,
but the days are so very long.

Noisy Newborns

I didn’t know newborns were so noisy,
with little grunts and groans.
I listen for your breath as you sleep,
interspersed with sighs and moans.

Losing weight

You've lost weight again,
I don't know what to do.
You need to get more milk
but I feel like I'm always feeding you.

I clearly am producing milk,
it leaks all over the place.
But you aren't getting enough, and
the worry shows on the midwife's face.

Maybe you have a tongue tie
or just don't know what to do.
I'm trying different positions,
but we really need a breakthrough.

The midwives told me hospital admission,
would be normal in a case this severe.
But the pandemic is all around us,
so we will have to resolve it here.

They say breastfeeding is natural.
The healthiest for you and me.
But I had no idea when I started,
how difficult it would be.

I feel the pressure building.
I'm letting my baby down.
I'm the only one who can feed him,
I feel that I might drown.

I collapse on the bathroom floor
while salty tears flow and drop.
I was determined I was going to breastfeed,
but the fear and pressure don't stop.

Slowly, I feel the tide is turning,
you're finally starting to grow.
But that fear is deep in my core now,
I'm not sure it'll ever go.

Advice

How do I know what's normal?
How do I know who to trust?
It's my first time being a mum.
Every sentence starts with, "You must..."

But each time, it's different.
No two pieces of advice the same.
So, I've decided to try and trust myself,
and the anxiety I work to tame.

Breastfeeding

Don't give up on a bad day,
somebody said to me.
But breastfeeding is much harder,
than I ever thought it would be.

Don't give up on a bad day,
I know this phase will pass.
He's still so tiny in my arms
and feels as fragile as glass.

Don't give up on a bad day,
but he's losing so much weight.
I seem to have plenty of milk,
but he doesn't know how to take.

Don't give up on a bad day,
but what if every day feels bad?
I sit here alone in the dark again
and fear I'm going mad.

Don't give up on a bad day
while my skin feels like it's crawling.
For every single touch and pinch
my tolerance is falling.

Don't give up on a bad day,
but he's just bitten again.
The most tender part of my body
is at the mercy of the pain.

Don't give up on a bad day,
is this the right thing to do?
The pressure is overwhelming,
I just want what's best for you.

Don't give up on a bad day.
Sometimes, it seems to click.
Snuggled up in my arms,
I give you goodness with every sip.

Don’t give up on a bad day,
it’s been two and a half years now.
I’m proud of gifting my milk to you,
but I’m not sure I‘ll miss it somehow.

Fourth Trimester

I've set your cot up by my bed,
a safe space just for you.
But you only want to sleep in my arms
no matter what I do.

I rock you close to me
and wait until you fall asleep.
But you sense it the moment
I try to lay you on your sheets.

These first few weeks have been exhausting,
sleep twenty minutes at a go.
I knew you were going to need me,
but I had no idea I'd feel so low

They call it the fourth trimester,
a time when baby needs to be near.
I am settling into the rhythm,
trying to be present with you here.

I hurt, ache and am bleeding still
exhausted from your birth.
But despite this, our bond is growing
in your first few weeks on earth.

A New Baby

When you go to meet a new baby,
please don't forget about Mum.
Check that she's ready for visitors,
before you make plans to come.

She may be feeling protective.
An instinct to keep her child close.
So, ask before you take baby,
show that you respect her thoughts the most.

She may be sore and exhausted
and relish the chance to rest.
Ask what you can do to help her
feel just a little bit less stressed.

She may not want to discuss the birth,
may still be processing it all.
But, this may be her first opportunity,
to have a really good, long bawl.

She may be worried about germs,
so please do wash your hands.
May not know what life looks like now,
so don't pressurise plans.

When you go to meet a new baby,
please don't forget about Mum.
There's a lifetime to bond with little one,
and right now, Mum might just feel numb.

Babies Not Here

TW: Miscarriage
& Infertility

I sit here for a moment,
with you cuddled close to me,
and think of all the babies
who never managed to be.

So many hearts are haunted
by that awful unspoken grief.
Trying not to drown in,
the loss of life so brief.

This time will be different,
I repeated endlessly in my mind.
But of course, there are no guarantees.
To higher powers, your fate is resigned.

But here you are, my rainbow.
A miracle sent to me.
Your life a celebration, finally,
of everything that can be.

And I think of all those mothers
who are still fighting every day.
Through infertility and loss.
Whose pain we can't take away.

I hope you find true peace,
and comfort along the way.
We stand together with you
and for your happiness, we pray.

Vacant Eyes

I feel like I could drown.
In this new role I find myself in.
Always feel like I am failing,
but suddenly, you show a grin.

At last, you seem to understand,
no longer have vacant eyes.
You smile and giggle with me,
I hope that stays throughout our lives.

Smiles

You smiled at me this morning,
waiting until I looked at you.
Your eyes focused across the room,
and lit up at the view.

You suddenly engage with me,
in a whole new range of ways.
No longer an expressionless bundle
from those very early days.

I thought I loved you fully,
but that bond has grown again.
My little baby so wonderful,
a light in the daily mundane.

Names

You said your first word today,
and unsurprisingly, it was "Cat."
He is your favourite thing in the world,
so, I was kind of expecting that.

You said "Dada" to your dad today,
with a beaming, great, big smile.
You haven't ever called me anything,
I've been waiting for a while.

I guess we're always together,
never spend any time apart.
So, you have no reason to greet me,
because you're always close to my heart

I had to go to the hospital today
with a terrible asthma attack.
My body ached from missing you so
when I returned, you shouted, "Cat!"

For six months, you called me "Cat."
Which I didn't mind a bit.
You loved the cat so much,
on my lap, you both would sit

Then suddenly, one dark morning,
you looked me straight in the eye,
called me "Mama" with a smile
and with tears in my eyes, I said, "Hi!"

Reflections

At times, I see glimpses of me in you,
and it catches me by surprise.
I know I grew you in my tummy,
but I didn't realise I'd see myself,
reflected in your eyes.

Army Crawl

You slither flat on your tummy,
like a soldier on the floor.
No interest in hands and knees,
I wonder if you'll ever crawl.

Your method is very effective.
It seems to work well for you.
Crossing the room in seconds,
when the cat comes wandering through.

Centre Of Attention

You're the centre of attention,
everywhere we go.
Whenever someone smiles at you,
your eyes light with a glow.

You flirt with every, single,
new waitress that you meet.
It didn't take you long to work out,
that they bring nice things to eat.

Despite being a lockdown baby,
behind closed doors hidden away.
You're a social little butterfly,
and so ready to explore and play.

Not Just A Mum (I)

I'm not just a mum, I realise,
but a teacher of rights and wrongs.
Narrator of stories and rhymes,
and performer of cheerful songs.

A cook, a dietitian, a tempter,
to try out new foods and tastes.
An artist's assistant with pens and paints,
a cleaner of glittery pastes.

I'm a persistent laundry warrior
with piles of washing on the floor.
A nappy changer, bath maker, nail clipper,
and the parent you always ask for.

I'm a tantrum-tamer and boundary-holder.
My arms creating a safe space.
Playmate, toy mender, book reader,
somebody to tickle and chase.

I'm your pillow and source of comfort,
when your tiny body is full of flu.
Your detective and investigator,
when you've lost something dear to you.

I'm your comforter, holding you gently,
when nightmares haunt you at night.
Mediator to help you share and be kind
when a tempting toy results in a fight.

I organise and lead great adventures.
Buy you ice cream in a cone.
Splash in puddles in the pouring rain.
Make sure you're never alone.

I support you to be brave and try.
Reassure when something goes wrong
Show you how to be kind,
and how in your loving family you belong.

You see, I'm not "just" a mum, really,
I try to do all that it takes.
Roles and responsibilities so endless.
A full-time job with no sick leave or breaks.

But I wouldn't change it for a minute.
Even though I'm exhausted to my core.
Being your mother is my priority now,
I am yours forever more.

Drowning

I feel like I've been drowning,
desperately gulping for air.
I've finally reached the surface,
but I'm not sure exactly where.

It's clear I've been drifting,
a long time in this rough sea.
As I lift my head now,
I just don't recognise me.

I fear I've lost my identity,
and path along the way.
It's exhausting constantly fighting
this rough sea every day.

Do I swim back towards
the places I have been?
Would I even recognise
all those things that I have seen?

If I swim forward,
will I reach a brand-new shore?
How do I know which of these
horizons I need to swim for?

Maybe I'll float and just
rest here for a while.
Let the calm sea carry me,
and save strength for the next trial.

Ashamed

I sometimes felt ashamed
when you asked, “What do you do?”
I didn’t have a job,
nothing to say to impress you.

But what if being a Mummy
is a valuable job, too?
And a huge responsibility,
to guide a soul so new.

Sacrifices

I have made so many sacrifices, caring for our child.

My body is still not recovered, my career lies in tatters.

I have lost myself completely, in the demands of every day.

But the one thing I can see clearly, is that my son is all that matters.

Identity

I fear I've lost my identity.
It's hard to decipher me.
I've spent so long surviving,
I only wanted to be free.

Where do I fit in the world?
Is there something I can not see?
Why do I feel locked away?
Should I be looking for a key?

Maybe I don't need answers yet.
I just don't know who I'll be.
It seems that I have healing to do,
before I can rediscover me.

Default Parent

Yes, I'm the default parent,
all the planning comes from me.
I'm responsible for everything,
but do you know how exhausting it can be?

Keeping the calendar updated,
find something for our tea.
Ensure the laundry's flowing,
how much more stuff can there be?

The house is always messy,
I don't have time to clean.
Our child is running wild.
What does it all mean?

It means I'm doing everything I can,
to keep us all together.
Everyone knows that they're loved, and
it won't last forever.

Single Mum

I didn't know I'd be a single mum
I didn't know it would be so hard
I worry that I'm failing you
I didn't know we'd be so scarred

I love you with all my heart,
I'm glad that we are free.
To live our lives side by side.
You're the best thing that happened to me.

I'm Sorry

I'm sorry that I judged you
when I was still so young.
I didn't know how hard it was
to be a single mum.

I'm sorry that I judged you,
when your kids were running around,
or noisily tantrumming,
while lying on the ground.

I'm sorry that I judged you,
when you looked so tired and spent.
I had no idea how sleep-deprived
you were, worrying about the rent.

I'm sorry that I judged you,
that first time that we met.
I realise now some marriages end,
when mothers escape great threat.

I'm sorry that I judged you
and believed society.
That mothers have to be perfect,
something I now fail to be.

Separated

Mummy doesn't live with Daddy.
We don't all live together.
She says being separate worked out best for us,
but that they'll both love me forever and ever.

Hope

In the darkest of moments,
lift your head and look around,
because it's when hope is waning,
that the light of love is found.

Balance

What does balance look like?
When I know you'll always be,
the greatest priority,
there will ever be for me.

How do I get my life back
and find a path to follow?
When I've lost myself entirely, and
my past now feels so hollow.

Easy Life

They told me life would be easy.
That I could have it all.
If I just played my part,
worked hard and dutifully played ball.

The problem, though, is that I'm a woman,
and what is expected of me.
Is actually impossible to achieve,
there is no way it can be.

If I work full-time, I'm "neglecting my child"
and struggling with nursery fees.
If I stay at home, I'm "depriving my child"
and am not the role model they should see.

Life in a loveless marriage,
is bad for my child, it's clear.
But the judgement faced by a single mum
just surrounds her with shame and fear.

Each mother makes her own choices,
and should be supported for doing so.
All that matters is her child is healthy,
plays and has a safe space to grow.

I'm Sorry That I Snapped

I'm sorry that I snapped today.
I know you did nothing wrong.
Sometimes, it's hard to explain,
how it feels to be a mum.

I love spending time with you,
but I struggle with the whining.
I never have a moment to myself,
over me, you're always climbing.

When did going to the bathroom
become a group activity?
I've been playing with you all morning,
but there's no time just to be me.

Your fingers crawl across my skin,
and feel like little mites.
My body is so touched out
each knock feels like a hammer smites.

You're full of energy all day,
which for a four-year-old is just right.
But we've both been up since dawn
and four times in the night.

Bedtime is a battle of wills.
You fight sleep every minute.
I just want to curl up into a ball,
I've reached every single limit.

I wouldn't change it for the world,
even though the days are long.
I do sometimes struggle through, but,
it's an honour to be your mum.

Your Toys

Your toys cover the entire floor.
There are clothes in tall, steep towers.
Your half-eaten breakfast,
is sitting going sour.

You weed into a closed drawer today,
I'm not sure how you managed!
You knocked three plants off a shelf,
there wasn't too much damage.

Life with you is chaotic.
You don't stop for breath all day.
But I know I wouldn't have it,
any other way.

Mess

The flat's a mess, as usual.
There are toys all over the floor.
It doesn't matter how much I tidy them.
Tomorrow, there'll just be more.

Cold Hard Stare

You really have developed,
an unsettling cold hard stare.
You've practised it daily in your pram
until its as good as a Peruvian bear.

You seem to reserve it for ladies,
who coo and fuss over you.
Shut down in a single moment,
as over your brows thunderclouds brew.

You don't back down for a second.
There's no thaw or sign of a smile.
The friendlier that they are to you,
the more you seem hostile.

It always makes me laugh,
because most of the rest of the time,
your face is lit with a smile,
as bright as summer sunshine.

I don't know what it is,
about friendly grannies that you mistrust.
But you keep on practising your glare
and by now it's full of disgust.

Nosy

Why are grownups so nosy?
So many questions every day!
Haven't they got stuff to get on with?
Why can't they just leave me to play?

What am I doing with that stepladder?
Where did that glue come from?
Why is there paint on the toilet?
When did the brown letter come?

Why are all the books on the floor?
When did I get spaghetti in my hair?
Who knocked over this plant pot?
How did that get up there?!

Your credit card? It's a mystery!
Who put the stapler in your bed?
Don't they know I'm very busy?
Couldn't they ask someone else instead?

But we can all weaponise questions.
I'll get my own back; just wait.
I'll keep asking "WHY?" repeatedly.
It never fails to make them irate!

Banana Drama

On Monday, I peeled the banana,
and sliced it into a bowl.
But turns out that was a disaster,
you wanted it still whole.

On Tuesday, I didn't slice it,
I left it as it came.
You stomped your foot and demanded
I sliced it up again.

On Wednesday, I slipped up early,
by opening the banana skin.
I didn't realise you wanted to open it,
I find myself trying to seal it back in.

On Thursday, I cautiously offer a banana,
but you said you hated them now.
You'd rather have an apple, you say,
I should feed them to a cow.

[Where would I find a cow?
They don't eat bananas, I'm pretty sure.
But anyway, I've got distracted,
there's more of this saga to endure.]

On Friday, you liked bananas again,
but you wanted them in long sticks.
I prepared it very carefully.
You only took two licks.

Today, I don't know what to try.
I had no idea before becoming a mum.
The drama surrounding bananas,
and how many ways I could prepare them wrong!

Gravity

I've come to the conclusion,
that you strongly believe,
gravity is a conspiracy,
only us grownups can perceive.

You seem very surprised,
when you fall with a thud,
having let go with both hands,
high above the mud.

When a wonky tower of blocks,
topples with a loud crash.
You seem almost insulted,
even though you gave it a bash.

You roll your eyes each time
somebody says, "be careful now".
Then, trip over a patch of thin air,
and fall hard down to the ground.

You're an experimental learner,
and you usually catch on quite quick.
But gravity still confounds you,
I think you feel it's a mean trick.

One day, you'll accept gravity,
as something that affects us all.
Until then, I'll be here to comfort you,
each time it makes you fall.

Bedtime

No one is busier than a toddler at bedtime,
there is suddenly so much to do.
Pencils to sharpen, a bridge to fix,
find all the animals from the zoo.

There are books to be read, snacks to be eaten,
and feathers to stick down with glue.
But most important is the surgery to open,
for a bear with a bad case of flu.

Peace In The Forest

I'm climbing the walls,
jumping on my bed.
Throwing myself off the sofa,
with a bump on my head.

I'm winding my mum up,
refusing to eat.
Chasing the cat,
and drumming my feet.

I'm screeching and squealing,
pulling Mum's hair.
Throwing my toys,
avoiding her glare.

I've been cooped up inside,
I'm going round the bend
All I really want,
is this imprisonment to end.

Please will you help me?
I don't want to be.
This big grumpy monster,
it just isn't me.

I want to jump in puddles,
look at the trees.
Balance on logs.
and scrape both my knees.

I want to run through the forest,
to eat on the floor
Look under large logs
and then run some more.

It might be raining,
sure there's an icy blast.
But I crave an adventure,
and freedom at last

Wrap me up warm,
put a flask in the car
Pack a warm blanket,
and let me go far.

Home in the evening,
I'll do what I'm asked.
I've found some peace in the forest
and I'll settle now, at last.

Big Day Out

We had a big day out today.
An expensive trip to the zoo.
So many incredible animals to see,
and great activities to do.

We saw tigers and elephants.
Even a mummy bear with her cub.
But it turns out your favourite part today,
was drinking melted ice cream from a tub.

Boo

When you were a tiny bean in my tummy,
I referred to you as Boo.
I didn't think much about it.
It just seemed the natural thing to do

Even though you're so big now.
From that little bean, you grew and grew.
I still find myself referring to you,
My darling, from my heart, as Boo.

Parents

Now that I'm a mother,
I see my parents in a new light.
Appreciate the hard choices they made,
for a future of hope and light.

TW: Loss of a loved one

Great Grandma

My Mummy had a Grandma,
she was my Grandma's Mum.
I wish I'd spent time with her,
she sounds so very fun.

Apparently, she loved to bake cakes,
and taught my Mum to cook.
She had a beautiful little garden,
and read stories from a book.

Mummy looks both sad and happy,
when she talks about her Grandma.
Mum says it's because she loved her so much,
but now she feels very far.

She says we couldn't visit her Grandma,
when I was very small.
Because of something called a pandemic,
but we talked often on video call.

It seems important to spend time,
with the people that we love.
We don't know when they'll go away,
but maybe she's watching from above.

Mummy said her Grandma
was thrilled when I was born.
But I bet she's also proud of my Mum,
and all the love that she adorns.

Deep Emotions

You feel such deep emotions,
it breaks my world apart.
When your cheeks streak with tears, my love.
You feel things so deep in your heart.

But you also feel joy so intensely.
It lights your face until you glow.
Your laughter is so infectious, dear.
Keep hold of that glee as you grow.

Riptide

Sometimes, I fear I'm losing you,
like a riptide out to sea.
Until bedtime comes around,
and you snuggle close to me.

Quiet

The flat is so quiet when you're not here.
Sounds echo as something falls to the floor.
I hear the whispers of your laugh in the quiet.
Remembered events from when you were small.

I miss you so much, my darling.
Our separation feels so unfair.
I walk to your bed in the middle of the night,
but realise that you're just not there.

I can't wait to have you back in my arms,
and I'll hold you close to me.
I guess this distance helps me realise,
how special our bond will be.

I won't ever stop you from seeing your dad,
while it's something you still want to do.
But I'll always be here to welcome you home,
I have nothing but love for you.

Nightmares

I hate when you have nightmares.
It feels like there is nothing I can do,
but sit beside you, hold your hand,
and tell you that I love you.

First Day

You had your first day at school today,
I can't believe it's already time.
It feels like only a moment ago,
you were a newborn covered in slime.

You were so brave and walked straight in,
not pausing with doubt for a second.
I'm so proud of how well you adapt,
when these new experiences beckon.

But today isn't just a big day for you,
it's a milestone for me as well.
I now have a son old enough for school,
to your toddler years, we bid farewell.

So, what do I do with myself now,
all the time that you're at school?
Can I start to rebuild my life somehow?
It feels like it's been unravelling from a spool.

First, I'm going to stop and take a breath.
Give myself a chance to remember and note.
All that we have overcome and survived.
How I've kept us safe and afloat.

We have been through so much together,
and this is a huge milestone to mark.
I'm so proud of our journey to this point,
and on many more adventures hope we embark.

Divorce

Divorce isn't just about sad endings.
It's the start of new beginnings, too.
To put everything that's happened far behind you,
and discover a brand new you.

Healing

Do you think we ever heal fully,
from the things that we've overcome?
Or does it stay deep inside us
leaving us doubting every outcome?

Maybe it makes us stronger.
Knowing we're resilient and survived.
Giving us context for future decisions.
A sense of freedom newly revived.

I think maybe it's up to us,
to take control of the trauma somehow.
To live life to its fullest and
it's negative influence no longer allowed.

But that's easier said than done,
and the most important thing.
Seems to be to trust yourself completely,
and be open to what the world will bring.

Single Parent

I suddenly realised I'm not afraid,
to walk this road alone.
I know I can keep you safe,
and build a loving home.

And Now?

So, what are you going to do now?
Someone asked me the other day.
I stumbled and paused for a lifetime,
I had no idea what to say.

I've been so focused on keeping us together.
On helping you learn and grow strong.
I've forgotten all about my dreams.
I'm no longer sure where I belong.

So now you've started at your school,
maybe I can dare to dream.
I'll have time to plan for my future,
and rebuild my lost self-esteem.

Pushing Boundaries

I'm starting to push my boundaries.
Challenging myself to do more.
Feeling the anxiety and embracing it,
to try things I've never done before.

It's not that the fear has gone.
It's as strong as it ever was.
But now I trust that I'm resilient,
and will survive whatever comes.

Friends

I'd missed having female friends,
who I could speak honestly to.
Revealing details from our lives,
letting someone else know you.

Giggling about the crush,
and sharing parenting stories.
It's nice to vocalise where I am
and identify this week's worries.

But the most rewarding thing,
from these interactions we share.
Is when they tell me something personal
and I can show that someone cares.

Butterflies

I get butterflies in my stomach
and lose all of my words.
When I see you walk towards me,
my response feels so absurd.

It's so long since I've felt this way.
Felt that blush rise on my face.
Struggling to say anything.
Drawn into your personal space.

I don't know if it's mutual,
If you feel the same as me.
But it has been a nice reminder,
that someone could be attracted to me.

Finding My Voice

I'm trying to find my voice
a way to express the real me.
But it's hard when it's been decades,
since my voice was last truly free.

I like to sit and listen quietly,
there's always so much to learn.
But I need to find a way to speak
when in the conversation, it's my turn.

I don't want to be the loudest voice,
or say things just for a reaction.
I'm not interested in defending myself,
in every single interaction.

It's important to me to be kind,
to treat people with respect,
Though, that doesn't mean always agreeing
or saying what I think they expect.

Writing seems to help the words
find clarity and escape from my head.
Those who share common ground seem to
understand why I've said what I've said.

I try to lower this stubborn mask,
relax the filter on each thought.
I don't need to censor myself anymore,
with the constant fear of being caught.

Years of intimidation and judgement
made my voice shrink and hide away.
Keeping myself safe was the priority,
but that danger is no longer here today.

So, I made myself a promise.
To find a voice that's truly me.
Exercise my freedom of speech,
and let my words flow, genuine and free.

I'm Proud

I'm proud of all you have achieved.
The challenges that you've overcome.
I know you've tried your hardest.
I see all that you have done.

I know you've had your battles,
have stumbled along the way.
Made mistakes and had misunderstandings,
but that really is OK.

It's alright darling, I realise,
that you're a long way from home.
So far, from all the people
and places that you have known.

I see you're shy and anxious,
each time you meet new souls.
Not sure where you fit in,
or who's playing which of the roles.

Your giggle is so infectious,
when you do let down your guard.
Laughter and mischief so natural
and straight from your little heart.

I can't protect you from the monsters,
or shield your heart from loss.
But I know you're strong and resilient,
into darkness, you'll never cross.

I feel your presence ever with me.
In the shadows and the light.
You're always there beside me,
as I lie awake in the night.

I see you,
I hear you,
I love you.
And with you, I'll always be.
We walk together on this path.
As my inner child and me.

TW: DV

What If?

What if "people pleaser" was coined
by someone who isn't kind?
What if "attention-seeker" by those
who've never known panic in their mind?

What if my strength was measured by
how much I was authentically me?
What if my happiness judged on
the wealth of my creativity?

What if our differences were met
with curiosity, not hate?
What if my worth was based
on my thoughts and not my weight?

What if my emotions were accepted,
as a normal part of life?
What if no one cared if my partner
was a husband or a wife?

What if I felt safe when I walked,
home alone in the dark?
What if I'd thought they'd believe me,
each time he left his mark?

What if my wrinkles and imperfections,
weren't something I had to hide?
What if my post-baby body,
was celebrated with great pride?

What if I didn't identify myself.
as "just a single mum"?
What if I relaxed a bit and
let myself have some fun?

What if you were more often quiet
and listened with pure intent?
What if every compliment you made
was true and genuinely meant?

What if I'm defined by what I love,
and not whether you love me?
What if I could start again and
create my own new reality?

Not Just A Mum (II)

I'm not just a mum, I realise.
I've grown from that starting place.
Found my voice and identity slowly.
A new version of me to embrace.

Of course, being your mother
is still so important to me.
Something I strive to give my all.
A priority it will always be.

But I'm a performer, a writer, a poet,
a photographer in love with nature.
An explorer and life documenter.
Someone open to fun and adventure.

I'm a lover, a friend and a daughter,
I have so much more to give.
A business that's mine to run,
and a life of my own to live.

I have dreams, hopes and ambitions.
Wish for a house and garden of our own.
Places I want to visit in the world.
To continue healing as I have grown.

I'm not just a mum I realise,
I have a life and story to tell.
And I'm so glad I get to share it with you,
as we both thrive, happy and well.

Change The World

I'm ready to change the world,
with a calm and gentle voice.

Share compassion and empathy,
with authenticity and grace.

I'm free to speak my truth,
and what a privilege that is.

It's time to make a difference,
in this world in which I live.

Arthur

It hasn't been easy darling.
There have been days I've not known what to do.
But I'd repeat it all in a heartbeat,
as it means a lifetime together with you.

Thank You

A huge thank you to everyone who has supported me along this journey, including my parents, Emilie, the chapel poets, everyone at Words Out Loud and of course my gorgeous son Arthur.

This collection of poems would never have seen the light of day without your support and encouragement. I will forever be in your debt.

Keep In Touch

Thank you so much for reading this book. It has been an emotional project for me, and I'm really honoured to share it with you. I am already working on another two collections which I hope to publish soon.

If you would like to read more of my poetry and keep up to date with news and events you can find me on Substack with username @KatieGowersIsFree or online at www.katiegowers.co.uk.

About The Author

Katie Gowers is a poet who writes about a wide range of topics including motherhood, mental health and stories for children. She began writing for herself to process difficult events in her life. She credits joining a writing group for the confidence to share her work both in written form and in regular performances at spoken word events. This is her first poetry collection to be published but she is already working on two more. She lives in Chichester, UK with her young son.

To find out more about Katie and her latest projects visit www.katiegowers.co.uk.

Image Credits

Background photograph of cover image licensed from lishanskyphotography at Getty Images.

Heart pattern licensed from lesichkadesign through canva.com

www.ingramcontent.com/pod-product-compliance
Ingram Content Group UK Ltd.
Pitfield, Milton Keynes, MK11 3LW, UK
UKHW050706170225
4621UKWH00052B/632

9 781068 356308